Visual Identification Series

The ABCs Field Guide to Young and Small Tree Pruning

Andrew G. Pleninger
and
Christopher J. Luley, Ph.D.

URBAN FORESTRY LLC
UrbanForestryLLC.com

Visual Identification Series, The ABCs Field Guide to Young and Small Tree Pruning

ISBN 978-0-9767129-2-3

CONTENTS

iv **PREFACE**

1 **SECTION A | ABOUT THIS GUIDE**
2   What is the ABCs Field Guide to Young & Small Tree Pruning?
4   Introduction to the ABCs Field Guide

7 **SECTION B | BRING YOUR TOOLS**
8   Gather Your Tools
10 Terminology
12 Pruning Cut Types
14 Removal Cut Objectives
16 Reduction and Heading Cut Objectives
18 Removal Cut Procedure – Branches with a Branch Collar
20 Removal Cut Procedure – Branches without a Branch Collar or Branch Bark Ridge
24 Reduction Cut Procedure
26 Heading Cut Procedure
28 Pruning Cut Tips

31 **SECTION C | START PRUNING – THE ABCs METHOD**
32 A – Assess the Tree – Determining The Pruning Dose
36 A – Assess the Tree – Tree Structure & ABCs Pruning Forms
40 A – Apical Dominance Pruning – A-Form Trees Only
44 B – Bad Branches
48 B – Bad Branch Attachments
50 C – Competing Branches – Clearance/Branching Height
54 C – Codominant Stems
56 C – Competing Laterals
58 C – Multiple Attachments – Horizontal Spacing
60 C – Vertical Spacing
62 C – Crossing Branches

65 **SECTION D | OTHER IMPORTANT PRUNING TIPS**
66 Timing of Pruning
68 Pruning Interval
70 Pruning Wound Dressing and Treatments
72 The DON'TS of Tree Pruning

75 **SECTION E | EXTRAS**
76 Determining a Branching Height
80 Using the ABCs – Before & Afters
85 ABCs Flow Chart

Pruning methodologies used today often ask the pruner to "imagine" what the tree should look like, and can be very technical. The ABCs emphasizes pruning the tree in front of you, and provides just enough technical background to help you understand how to prune.

Preface

Each year, significant time and expense is dedicated to tree maintenance – the majority of which involves tree pruning. As arborists and trained observers, we see the results of improper tree pruning every day. In addition, we see that most young or small trees are not pruned by professional arborists, but rather by homeowners, municipal highway crews and ground maintenance workers who likely have little or no training in tree pruning.

As instructors, we have experienced the challenge of teaching proper tree pruning. While tree pruning is often called an art, we are certainly not artists or art teachers. However, a strictly scientific approach to tree pruning often results in glazed over looks from trainees. We recognized the need for a more practical and logical methodology for presenting and teaching pruning. We asked ourselves, "How much technical knowledge is necessary to properly prune a tree?"

We decided to create a pruning method that was easier to teach, learn and remember, and that addressed the pruning needs of most small and young trees. We identified what we believe to be the primary issues and challenges to successful pruning and tree maintenance. These topics and techniques became the foundation – the ABCs – of this Guide to teaching, learning and completing proper tree pruning.

Pruning young and small trees can be accomplished by anyone with the desire and the proper hand tools. The ABCs presents a simple stepwise method to pruning that anyone can follow and remember. If completed properly, it may increase the lifespan of a tree by eliminating common defects.

In order to properly prune small trees, a limited knowledge of the science behind tree pruning is necessary. We provide enough technical background to help you understand how to prune, without overwhelming you with scientific details.

Typical pruning methodologies used today ask the pruner to "imagine" what the tree should look like, or to prune to an idealized set of protocols.

The ABCs is a step-by-step methodology that logically identifies where to start and when to stop pruning, and also provides a sequence that is easy to recall in the field.

Our protocols for making pruning decisions are instead based on observation of the tree in front of you, and then focusing on what can be done to improve the health and structure of that particular tree.

Maintenance pruning is not an art. Therefore, it requires a methodology for use in the field that logically leads the pruner through branch pruning decisions, identifies where to start and when to stop pruning, and is easy to recall. The ABCs guides the pruner from start to finish and helps ensure that pruning is completed properly on the majority of trees in the landscape.

This Guide is designed for use on trees that can be pruned from the ground, although these principles can also be applied to larger trees. We believe that our structured, easily recalled methodology will help you improve the quality of your tree pruning efforts and provide you with the satisfaction of knowing that you have completed them properly.

Section A

About This Guide

Section A | About This Guide

What is the ABCs Field Guide to Young & Small Tree Pruning?

The ABCs is a systematic and prioritized method for proper tree pruning. It uses the ABCs acronym to guide you through the process and help you easily recall this method.

A – Assess the Tree

A – Apical Dominance Pruning (prune for a central stem)

B – Bad Branches
(dead, diseased, defective)

C – Competing Branches

D – Dose
(amount to prune)

Most young trees never receive proper pruning in spite of the fact that pruning:

▶ Requires minimal training to learn proper techniques.

▶ Requires little time to complete.

▶ Can be accomplished from the ground using hand tools.

▶ Can dramatically extend the useful life of trees in the landscape by eliminating life-shortening defects.

This Guide is intended for use on trees that can be pruned from the ground with hand tools. Tree climbing or use of a chain saw is not necessary or recommended. The Guide is intended for a wide range of users, from professionals to people who have little or no experience pruning trees.

The ABCs to pruning young and small trees begins with A – Assessing the tree.

A – Apical Dominance Pruning
Pruning begins with apical dominimance pruning, which includes pruning to promote a single central stem from the trunk to the top of the tree (on most trees).

B – Bad Branches
Bad branches to be pruned includes removal of branches with weak branch attachments to help avoid catastrophic branch failure later in the tree's life, as shown here.

C – Competing Branches
This includes pruning branches that create clearance issues or compete with one another by virtue of their size and location in the tree.

Introduction to the ABCs Field Guide

The ABCs Field Guide to Young & Small Tree Pruning will provide you with:

▶ Specific guidance on tool selection.

▶ Instruction on how to make and use different pruning cuts.

▶ A systematic, prioritized, easy-to-learn and easy-to-remember pruning methodology.

▶ A succinct guide for use in the field.

▶ A photographic and illustrated presentation with just enough supporting text.

Each ABCs topic is presented on a page or series of pages and is divided and organized into the following four sections:

1. **Introduction**
   Definition and description of the topic.

2. **Objectives**
   Learning objectives for the topic.

3. **Application**
   Specific instructions for applying the topic.

4. **Pictures & Illustrations**
   Visual examples and techniques of the topic.

5

Section A
Overview of the ABCs Field Guide

Section B
Gather Proper Pruning Tools
➤ Recommended pruning tools

Learn the Proper Pruning Cuts & Uses
➤ Removal Cut
➤ Reduction Cut
➤ Heading Cut

Section C
Execute the ABCs
➤ A – Assess the Tree
➤ A – Apical Dominance Pruning
➤ B – Bad Branch Pruning
➤ C – Competing Branch Pruning

Section D
Important Pruning Considerations
➤ When is the best time to prune and how often should a tree be pruned?
➤ Wound dressing?
➤ How many of the lower branches on the tree should be removed?

Section E
Extras
➤ Photographic before and after examples of ABCs pruning.

Section B

Bring Your Tools

Section B | Bring Your Tools

Gather Your Tools

Before you start pruning, make sure you have the proper pruning tools. The use of quality tools is highly recommended, as low quality tools perform poorly. High quality tools allow the pruner to make "clean" cuts that cause the least amount of injury to the tree, and require the least physical effort. The tools we recommend are described and pictured in the next few pages. If a tool is not discussed here it is either not required, or we do not recommend its use.

Tool Types

Pruning tools are classified into two basic types: pruners and saws. The size and type of tool you choose is determined by the size and location of the branch to be cut. If a branch won't cut easily, is being twisted or ripped, or you are using excessive effort when pruning, you are most likely using the wrong tool.

OBJECTIVE

▶ Learn about the pruning tools we recommend, their application and use.

▶ Learn to match the right tool type with the size of the branch to be pruned.

APPLICATION
Collect the following tools and be sure they are clean and sharp:

Bypass (Scissor) Pruners
Three types of bypass pruners are required.

▶ Hand pruners for small branches (less than ½-inch diameter);

▶ Loppers (24-inch or longer handles) for branches up to 1½ inches in diameter; and

▶ Pole pruner for cutting branches up to 1½ inches in diameter that can't be reached from the ground.

Do not use anvil-style pruners; they crush branch tissues and do not provide a clean cut.

Saws
Most pruning saws cut on the pull stroke of the sawing action. Saws with smaller teeth and narrow tooth spacing are for cutting small diameter branches. They cut more slowly, but result in a cleaner cut. We recommend:

▶ Small folding saw with no larger than an 8-inch blade for cutting branches up to 2 inches in diameter.

Saws with larger teeth and wider spacing between the teeth are used for larger diameter branches. We recommend:

▶ Fixed-handle hand saw with a blade of no more than 15 inches.

▶ Same or similar blade size to be used on a pole pruner head.

Pole Pruner and Saw Sets

▶ For safety reasons, use poles made of wood or fiberglass that do not conduct electricity.

▶ Collapsible or two-section pole set with a minimum total length of 10 feet is sufficient.

For best results, we recommend professional-grade tools from high quality manufacturers, which can be found online at any arborist supply distributor.

Disinfectant

Pruning tools should be cleaned with a disinfectant after pruning diseased branches from a tree, to prevent spread of the disease. A $\frac{1}{10}$ solution of bleach/water (effective but corrosive), 95% rubbing alcohol, or a commercial disinfectant product (such as Physan 20 [physan.com]) in a spray bottle is a convenient method for cleaning a tool between pruning cuts.

▶ Clean the pruning tool after removing each diseased branch from a tree and before leaving a diseased tree.

Bypass hand pruner for branches less than ½-inch diameter.

Long-handled (24-inch) bypass lopper for branches up to 1½-inch diameter.

8-inch folding saw for branches up to 2-inch diameter.

13 to 15-inch fixed blade hand saw for 2-inch or larger branches.

Bypass pruner head on a pole pruner.

Fixed saw blade on a pole pruner.

Fiberglass or wood pole pruner and saw sets should have a minimum of 10 feet total reach. A fiberglass pole with a single section and a bypass pruner head is shown here.

Terminology

The majority of pruning terms are defined in the body of this guide. The following terms provide the foundation for completing the ABCs.

OBJECTIVE

▶ To learn the basic terminology for using the ABCs.

APPLICATION

▶ **Apical Dominance Pruning**
The pruning process of developing and maintaining the central stem throughout the height of the tree.

▶ **Branch Attachment**
The point where a scaffold, branch or twig originate and join together.

▶ **Branch Structure**
The general pattern, spacing and attachment of branches in a tree.

▶ **Central Stem**
The main stem starting from the trunk and first scaffold branch to the top of the tree.

▶ **Codominant Stems**
Two upward-growing stems of similar size and growth rate, which are attached or originating at the same location on the central stem.

▶ **Crown**
The collection of scaffolds, branches, twigs and leaves.

▶ **Lateral**
A branch originating from a larger branch, scaffold branch or the trunk.

▶ **Live Branch Area**
The sum of living branch tissue and leaves on a tree or an individual branch.

▶ **Multiple Branch Attachments**
Two or more branches or stems attached at the same location on the trunk or central stem.

▶ **Parent**
A stem or branch that bears smaller branches.

▶ **Root Crown**
The base of the tree where roots transition to the trunk.

▶ **Scaffold**
The largest diameter branch(s) attached to the trunk or central stem that give the tree its primary form and structure.

▶ **Sprout**
A small branch produced on the trunk or larger branches in response to branch removal, wounding or other stress.

▶ **Stem**
The woody trunk or a branch of a tree.

▶ **Sucker**
A small branch produced on the root collar.

▶ **Trunk**
The main stem from the root crown to the lowest scaffold or main branches.

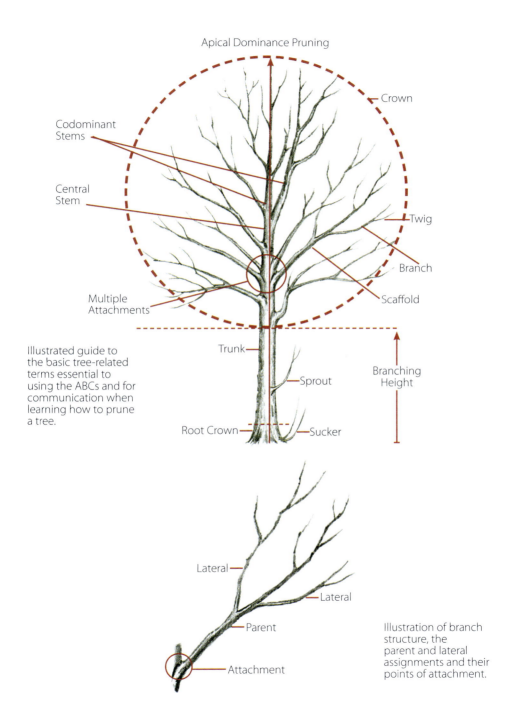

Apical Dominance Pruning

Crown

Codominant
Stems

Central
Stem

Twig

Branch

Multiple
Attachments

Scaffold

Illustrated guide to
the basic tree-related
terms essential to
using the ABCs and for
communication when
learning how to prune
a tree.

Trunk

Sprout

Branching
Height

Root Crown

Sucker

Lateral

Lateral

Parent

Illustration of branch
structure, the
parent and lateral
assignments and their
points of attachment.

Attachment

Pruning Cut Types

A pruning cut is one of the "tools" you use in tree pruning. The objective of a pruning cut is to remove a portion of the tree, such as a branch or a portion of a branch. Pruning cut types include removal, reduction and heading cuts.

No pruning cut should be made unless a specific objective is identified for making the cut.

The possible objectives of each cut type and how to make each cut are detailed in the remainder of this section.

OBJECTIVE

▶ Learn the three types of pruning cuts.

APPLICATION

▶ **Removal Cut**
Removes the entire branch at its point of origin.

▶ **Reduction Cut**
Shortens the parent to a lateral that is at least ⅓ the diameter of the parent.

▶ **Heading Cut**
Shortens the parent, but makes the final cut between laterals, or to a lateral that is less than ⅓ the diameter of the parent.

REMOVAL CUT

Removal cuts remove the branch at its point of origin.

HEADING CUT

Heading cuts shorten the length of the parent but the final cut may leave a stub or may be cut to a lateral that is less than ⅓ the diameter of the parent.

REDUCTION CUT

Branch is shortened

Lateral at least ⅓ the diameter of the parent

Parent

Reduction cuts shorten the parent to a lateral that is at least ⅓ the diameter of the parent.

Removal Cut Objectives

Removal cuts are made to meet several different pruning objectives. Removal cuts can have a significant impact on tree growth because they completely eliminate the branch and its energy-producing leaves. As a result, they can also have a positive or negative impact on tree health and appearance.

OBJECTIVE

▶ Learn the objectives for making removal cuts.

APPLICATION

Reasons to make removal cuts:

▶ To establish a single central stem in the tree or improve tree structure.

▶ To remove bad branches (Section B – Bad Branches)
  • Dead, diseased, pest-infested or broken branches.
  • Undesirable or defective branches.

▶ To remove competing branches. (Section C – Competing Branches)
  • Provide clearance for equipment, lighting or people.
  • Improve branch spacing and structure.

Removal cut on a branch with a poor branch attachment angle. (Section B – Bad Branches)

Removal cut is being made to eliminate a branch competing with the central stem (white line). (Section C – Competing Branches)

Removal cut being made to improve clearance under the tree. (Section C – Competing Branches - Clearance)

Removal cuts (arrows) were made to improve branch spacing and tree structure. (Section C – Competing Branches - Vertical Spacing)

Reduction and Heading Cut Objectives

Reduction and heading cuts are used to accomplish one or a combination of three objectives: branch growth suppression, to alter branch growth direction, and to reduce the amount of live branch tissue removed.

OBJECTIVE

▶ Learn the reasons for using reduction and heading cuts.

- **Branch Growth Suppression (Suppress)**
  Removing the terminal portion of a branch and the accompanying leaf area will suppress the growth of the pruned branch in several ways. First, removing energy-producing leaves will slow branch growth. Secondly, by removing a branch's terminal, growth in length of the branch will be slowed. The amount and duration of growth suppression is tied to the amount of live branch area removed.

- **Directing Branch Growth**
  If a branch is growing in an undesirable direction, removing the terminal portion of a branch can redirect growth to a lateral growing in the desired direction.

- **Reduce the Amount of Pruning**
  Reduction and heading cuts remove less live branch area than removal cuts, which allows for more pruning elsewhere on the tree.

APPLICATION

▶ Branch suppression:

- Remove ⅓ to ¾ of the live branch area of the branch depending on the desired growth suppression.
- Growth will be suppressed depending on how much live branch area is removed.

▶ Use reduction cuts when:

- The branch will be retained on the tree permanently or for an extended period of time.
- Removing the entire branch is undesirable due to its size.

▶ Use heading cuts instead of reduction cuts when:

- The branch will be removed at a later pruning event.
- Pruning small, vigorously growing branches.

A reduction cut being made to suppress a branch that is too large in diameter relative to the central stem (arrow) and is creating an aesthetically unbalanced form of the tree.

A heading cut being used to slow or suppress the growth of this branch which is competing with the selected central stem (white line). At least ⅓ of the live branch area of the branch must be removed to suppress its growth, more if suppression is desired for more than one year.

A reduction cut is being used to redirect the growth of this low branch to a lateral higher over a sidewalk and suppress its growth.

This crabapple has a lateral branch that is competing in size with the central stem and creating an unbalanced crown. Completely removing the branch would remove too much live branch area on the tree. A heading cut was used to suppress the growth of the branch (upper arrow).

Removal Cut Procedure – Branches with a Branch Collar

A removal cut removes a branch at its point of origin. A properly made removal cut takes advantage of the protective barriers present within stem and branch tissues and minimizes injury to the parent branch. On healthy trees, removal cuts will seal quickly and do not require further treatment such as wound dressings.

OBJECTIVE

▶ Learn how to make a proper removal cut and the terms that are essential to this procedure.

▶ Identify the branch collar or swelling at the base of a branch where it joins the trunk or parent branch.

▶ Identify the branch bark ridge or the raised area of bark in the branch attachment, marking where the branch and stem meet.

▶ Learn how to make a proper removal cut, respecting the branch collar and branch bark ridge.

APPLICATION

▶ To make a removal cut:

- Identify the branch collar and branch bark ridge.

  – If a branch collar or branch bark ridge is absent (see Removal Cut Procedure – Branches without Branch Collar or Branch Bark Ridge).

- Make the final cut just outside the branch collar and branch bark ridge.

▶ If the branch is dead, do not cut into the tissue or new growth (wound wood) that has formed around the old branch site.

▶ Removal cuts should not:

- Cut into the branch collar, branch bark ridge or parent branch.
- Leave a stub.
- Damage the parent branch or stem.

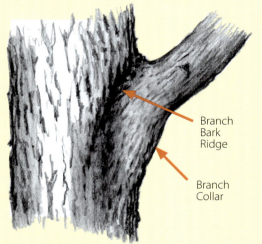

Branch
Bark
Ridge

Branch
Collar

Before making a removal cut, identify the branch collar and branch bark ridge.

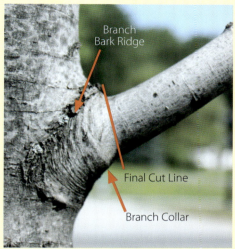

Branch
Bark Ridge

Final Cut Line

Branch Collar

The final cut is made outside the branch bark ridge and branch collar.

A properly made removal cut on branches with branch collars will begin to seal with wound wood (arrow), resulting in a complete ring around the wound.

Branch
Bark Ridge

Final
Cut Line

Wound
Wood

Branch
Collar

When pruning a dead branch, make the final cut without cutting the live wound wood tissue, the branch bark ridge or branch collar.

Removal Cut Procedure – Branches Without a Branch Collar or Branch Bark Ridge

The branch collar and branch bark ridge represent the location where there is a transition of internal wood from the parent stem to the lateral branch. On many branches, the branch collar and branch bark ridge are readily apparent. However, some branches do not have a recognizable branch collar or branch bark ridge, and identifying where to make the final pruning cut can be difficult. Additional care needs to be taken when making the final cut so as not to damage the parent stem during the branch removal.

OBJECTIVE

▶ Learn how to make the final cut on branches without a branch collar or branch bark ridge present.

APPLICATION

▶ Draw an imaginary line perpendicular (90 degrees) to the branch bark ridge or seam where the branches meet.

▶ Cut at approximately a 45 degree angle, bisecting (dividing equally) the 90 degree angle formed by the branch bark ridge or seam and the imaginary line (see illustration).

  • The exact angle of the final cut is less important than avoiding cutting into the parent branch or leaving a stub.

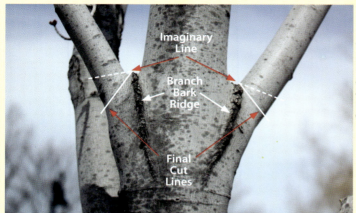

Imaginary
Line

Branch
Bark
Ridge

Final
Cut
Lines

Laterals without well-defined branch collars. Draw an imaginary line perpendicular (90 degrees) to the branch bark ridge where the branches meet. Make the final cut bisecting (dividing equally) the angle formed by the imaginary line and the branch bark ridge. Use care not to cut the branch bark ridge, damage the parent, or leave a stub.

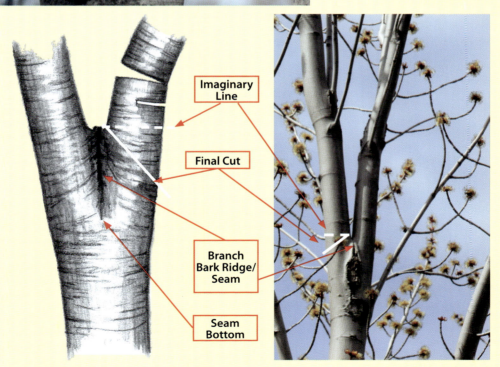

Imaginary
Line

Final Cut

Branch
Bark Ridge/
Seam

Seam
Bottom

Codominant stems often do not have a branch collar. Draw an imaginary line perpendicular (90 degrees) to the branch bark ridge or seam, starting where the stems meet. Make the final cut bisecting (dividing equally) the angle formed by the imaginary line and the seam, without cutting the branch bark ridge or seam. Do not extend the final cut below the bottom of the branch bark ridge or seam.

Final Cut Line (Cut from the bottom)

Seam

Parent

Branches without a branch bark ridge. Draw an imaginary line perpendicular (90 degrees) to seam starting where the branches meet. Make the final cut bisecting (dividing equally) the angle formed by the imaginary line and the seam. In this case, make the final cut starting on the underside of the branch cutting toward the parent.

Branch Collar

Conifer trees such as spruce, pine and larch usually have a visible branch collar. However, they rarely have a branch bark ridge. The final cut is made just outside the branch collar without cutting the parent or leaving a stub.

Reduction Cut Procedure

A reduction cut removes the end or terminal portion of a parent at a lateral that is at least ⅓ the diameter of the parent. Reduction cuts are used when removal of the entire branch is undesirable or unnecessary.

OBJECTIVE

▶ Learn how to make a proper reduction cut.

APPLICATION

To make a reduction cut:

▶ Select a suitable lateral for shortening the parent.

- The lateral should be at least ⅓ the diameter of the parent at its point of attachment.

- The remaining lateral should be growing in a desirable direction.

▶ Draw an imaginary line perpendicular to the branch bark ridge or seam where the parent and laterals meet.

- Make the final cut bisecting (dividing equally) the angle formed by the branch bark ridge or seam and the imaginary line.

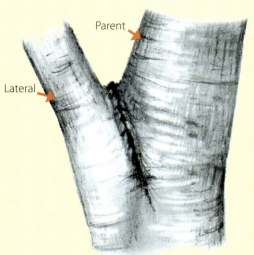

The lateral selected should be at least ⅓ the diameter of the parent.

A reduction cut removes the terminal portion of branch back to a lateral branch at least ⅓ the diameter of the parent branch. The lateral selected should be growing in a desirable direction.

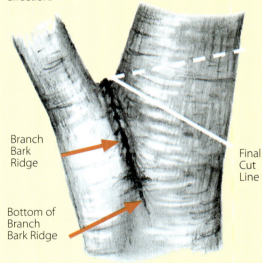

When making the final cut on a reduction cut, draw an imaginary line perpendicular (90 degrees) to the top of the branch bark ridge where the branches meet. Make the final cut bisecting (dividing equally) the angle formed by the imaginary line and the branch bark ridge, without the cutting the branch bark ridge. Do not extend the cut below the bottom of the branch bark ridge.

Select a lateral that is growing in the desired direction.

Heading Cut Procedure

A heading cut shortens or removes the end or terminal portion of a branch, like a reduction cut. However, the final cut is made between laterals, leaving a stub, or at a lateral less than ⅓ the diameter of the parent stem.

OBJECTIVE

▶   Learn how to make a heading cut.

APPLICATION

▶   Complete a heading cut by:

  • Cutting the branch to a location between lateral branches, leaving a stub, or

  • Cutting to a lateral less than ⅓ the diameter of the parent branch.

Heading cuts shorten a branch by removing the terminal portion of a branch. They are different from a reduction cut because they may leave a stub.

Lateral is less than ⅓ the diameter of the parent

Heading cuts also differ from a reduction cut because they can be made to a small lateral that is less than ⅓ the diameter of the parent.

Heading cuts may be used on difficult to reach small, vigorous branches high in the tree.

A heading cut being made to a lateral smaller the ⅓ the diameter of the parent.

Pruning Cut Tips

Several practical tips are described here to make pruning easier and safer, and to reduce potential damage to the tree. These are:

▶ Partially remove most of a branch first before making the final cut. This technique should be used on most branches to avoid struggling with the weight and length of a branch while making the final cut.

▶ Remove branches with narrow branch angles by cutting from the underside of the branch. This reduces potential damage to the parent branch in cases where the saw does not fit between the branch and parent stem.

▶ Cut tangled branches into pieces to remove them. Branches that are tangled in the tree can cause considerable damage to remaining buds, foliage or bark if they are pulled out in once piece after pruning.

OBJECTIVE

▶ Learn how to safely and properly remove any branch from a tree.

APPLICATION

▶ Remove most branches following this three-cut sequence;

- Make an undercut part of the way through the branch, at least six inches away from where it is attached. This prevents the branch from "ripping," damaging the parent branch.

- Cut entirely through the branch just beyond the partial cut (towards the end of the branch) and remove the majority of the branch.

- Make the final pruning cut, holding onto the remaining branch stub.

▶ Remove branches with narrow branch angles, where the saw does not fit between the branch and its parent, by cutting from the underside of the branch.

- Make the final cut with a saw, starting from the underside of the branch.

- Be sure to the make the cut at an angle that does not leave a stub or cut into the branch bark ridge.

▶ Remove tangled branches by cutting them into smaller segments and pulling them out without damaging other branches.

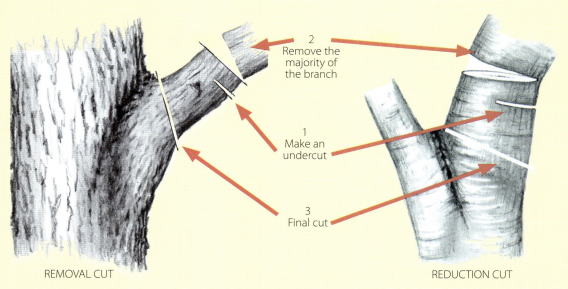

2
Remove the
majority of
the branch

1
Make an
undercut

3
Final cut

REMOVAL CUT   REDUCTION CUT

Three Step Method
Prune branches with three cuts; (1, 2 then 3) to minimize the risk of ripping and damaging the parent branch or damaging other branches in the tree.

Make your final cut cutting from the underside of the limb for branch angles that are too tight to fit the saw.

Tangled branches such as this branch should be removed in pieces to avoid damaging other branches in the tree. Start at the end of the branch, removing smaller pieces until the entire branch is removed.

Start Pruning –
The ABCs Method

Section C | Start Pruning – The ABCs Method

A: Assess the Tree – Determining the Pruning Dose

The pruning dose is the percentage of live crown you will prune from the tree during this pruning event. Tree health is used to determine the dose. Young trees and healthy trees can tolerate more pruning than newly planted, unhealthy or older trees. Dose is monitored closely when using the ABCs method and pruning is stopped when dose is reached. Over-pruning is a common pruning mistake. Determining, monitoring and adhering to a predetermined dose will help avoid this error.

OBJECTIVE

▶ Make an assessment of tree health and determine the pruning dose, using several visual indicators.

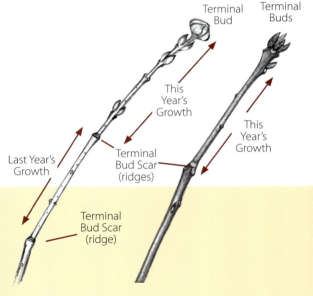

Terminal Bud

Terminal Buds

This Year's Growth

Last Year's Growth

Terminal Bud Scar (ridges)

This Year's Growth

Terminal Bud Scar (ridge)

Yellow or off-color leaves and dead branches throughout the tree are an indicator of poor health. This tree should only receive the low dose.

Annual Twig Growth
The terminal bud scar (ridges) encircling the twig (red lines) identify the termination of the previous year's growth. Select a minimum of three branches on the edge of the crown then measure the distance between these ridges starting from the end of a twig. If they are declining in length or less than three inches, this is an indicator the tree is in declining or poor health.

APPLICATION

▶ Determine tree health by observations of:
  • Leaf color and size relative to a normal tree of the same species.
  • Annual twig growth.
    – Inspect a number of twigs throughout the crown.
    – Twigs with less than three inches of annual growth is an indicator of poor or declining health.
  • Density of foliage.
  • Presence of dead, diseased or dying branches.

▶ Then, determine the prescribed pruning dose as follows:
  • Newly planted trees or those with significant deficiencies in any of the above categories:
    – Low Dose – Suppress for apical dominance, prune bad branches and head branches for clearance only.
  • No deficiencies or minor deficiencies in the health categories above:
    – Normal Dose – Prune up to 33% of the live crown.
  • Young trees that are growing vigorously (twig growth increments in excess of one foot):
    – High Dose – 33% of the live crown.
      Caution: Removing too much live crown may lead to tree decline or death. It is always best to err on the side of caution by removing less.

Annual twig growth on a silver maple illustrated by locating the terminal bud scars. The white arrows line up with the last three years' growth from left to right.

Continued on next page.

Low density of foliage is an indicator of poor health. This tree should only receive the low dose.

Presence of numerous dead or diseased branches is an indicator of poor health. This tree should receive the low dose.

Dose is the percentage of live crown removed during a pruning event. Dose should be monitored closely by piling the branches as you prune and quantifying the percentage of live crown removed during each ABCs pruning step.

Assess The Tree – Tree Structure & ABCs Pruning Forms

Assessing tree structure will include two tasks: classifying the tree into one of two pruning "forms" and identifying bad or competing branches in the tree that may need to be pruned. The latter will be more clearly defined in later sections.

There are two general tree pruning forms that are used in the ABCs: A-Form trees and B-Form trees. The majority of trees are A-Form. A-Form trees will be pruned to develop and maintain a single central upright stem that arises from the lowest branch on the tree to the top of the tree. B-Form (or broad or open form) trees are trees that do not have and/or will not be pruned to a single central stem. You will need to classify the tree into one of these two pruning forms prior to beginning pruning.

Pruning with the ABCs will result in a branching structure that is consistent with the tree's <u>present</u> and natural growth form.

OBJECTIVE

▶ Determine if the tree is an A or B Pruning Form.

▶ Inspect the tree for significant B – Bad Branches & C – Competing Branches that may need pruning (definitions will be provided in later sections).

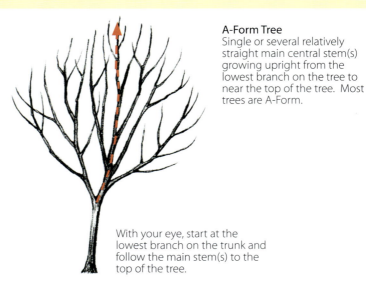

A-Form Tree
Single or several relatively straight main central stem(s) growing upright from the lowest branch on the tree to near the top of the tree. Most trees are A-Form.

With your eye, start at the lowest branch on the trunk and follow the main stem(s) to the top of the tree.

APPLICATION

Walk around the tree and observe the main structure of the tree.

▶ ABCs Pruning Form

- Visually, start at the lowest branch on the trunk and trace up the trunk of the tree, following the largest of the main stems to the termination of the stem.

  – If your path is upright, relatively straight in direction and you terminate near the very top of the tree, the tree is an A-Form.

  – If your path travels horizontally, includes nearly 90 degree or right angle turns, and more often than not terminates on a horizontal branch, the tree is a B-Form.

  – If your path can lead up many stems, starting at approximately the same point on the trunk, the tree is a B-Form.

- If the tree is an A-Form, proceed to Step A – Apical Dominance Pruning

- If the tree is a B-Form start with Step B – Bad Branches

▶ Identify any bad or competing branches that may need to be pruned.

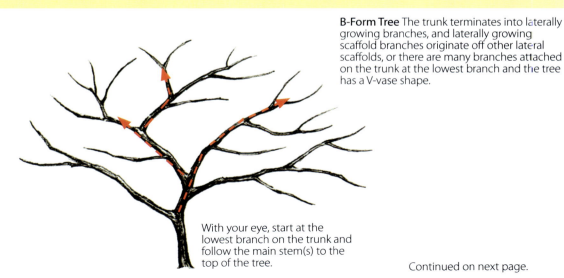

B-Form Tree The trunk terminates into laterally growing branches, and laterally growing scaffold branches originate off other lateral scaffolds, or there are many branches attached on the trunk at the lowest branch and the tree has a V-vase shape.

With your eye, start at the lowest branch on the trunk and follow the main stem(s) to the top of the tree.

Continued on next page.

This A-Form sycamore tree has a single central stem traveling from the lowest branch to the top of the tree.

This Norway maple has several upright growing stems competing to become the central stem. The largest of these stems leads you upright to the top of the tree and will serve as the central stem. The tree should be pruned as an A-Form tree.

Here, an ornamental hawthorn tree has a well-established central stem traveling from the lowest branch to the top of the tree, and therefore should be pruned as an A-Form tree.

B-Form
An ornamental
tree with multiple
horizontal scaffolds.

B-Form
Multiple scaffolds
originating from the
same point on the
trunk, giving the tree
a V-shape.

A – Apical Dominance Pruning – A-Form Trees Only

Apical dominance is the control exerted by the terminal growing point of a stem over the growth of lateral branches below it. The objective of this pruning step is to develop, promote and maintain a single central stem from the ground to the top of the tree. *This is the most critical step in pruning A-Form trees.*

OBJECTIVE

▶ Select a central stem.

▶ Identify and prune any branches competing with the central stem for apical dominance.

APPLICATION

▶ Identify or select the central stem.

- A single stem that starts at the lowest branch on the tree and terminates at the top of the tree.
- A collection of upright/relatively straight stems in the center of the tree that added together terminate at the top of the tree.

▶ Suppress branches competing with the central stem using heading cuts.

- Codominant stems that are attached to the central stem.
- Lateral branches that are competing with the central stem for apical dominance.
- Be sure to step back and observe if any lateral branches lower in the tree will compete with the central stem.

Measure your pruning dose by placing each branch pruned in a single pile and quantify the percentage of live crown removed.

▶ Stop pruning once dose is reached, or proceed to the next branch or step if dose has not been reached.

This maple tree has a single central stem starting at the lowest branch to the top of the tree. This is the most desirable tree structure. Apical dominance pruning works to suppress the growth of laterals and stems that are competing with a selected central stem.

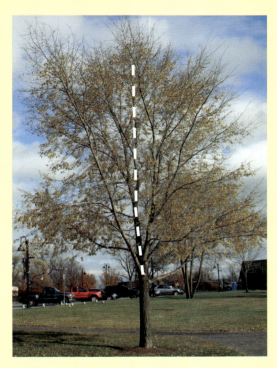

This elm has several upright stems that collectively will be selected to serve as the central stem.

Continued on next page.

Laterals competing (red arrows) for apical dominance with the central stem (white line) were suppressed.

Conifers can often produce stems competing for apical dominance. Select one as the central stem and head any stems competing with the central stem.

This codominant stem competing for apical dominance in this hackberry will be suppressed using a heading cut to promote growth of the central stem (white line).

A crabapple with a central stem (white line). A lateral (yellow arrow) is competing with the central stem and should be suppressed.

B – Bad Branches

Bad branches are branches that are dead, diseased or structurally defective. These branches are detrimental to the long-term health or structure of the tree.

OBJECTIVE

▶ Identify and prune all bad branches present in the tree.

▶ Take necessary sanitation precautions when infectious diseases are present.

APPLICATION

Locate any bad branches, including those that are:

▶ Dead, cracked or broken.

▶ Diseased – Have serious pests such as cankers, galls, or decay.

▶ Rubbing and damaging other branches.

Use removal or reduction cuts to eliminate bad branches.

▶ If an infectious disease is present, try to cut 12 inches below the diseased tissues if possible.

  • Disinfest pruning tools between cuts where infectious disease might be spread on tools.

  • Remove and burn or destroy diseased branches as soon as possible.

Measure your pruning dose by placing each branch pruned in a single pile and quantify the percentage of live crown removed.

▶ Stop pruning once dose is reached, or proceed to the next branch or step if dose has not been reached.

Broken, split or severely damaged branches should be removed.

Dead branches should be removed. Do not cut the wound wood or branch collar when making the final cut.

Branch stubs should be removed.

Continued on next page.

Diseased Branches – Blights
Blights may be identified by the discoloring of leaves and branch tissue or death of the tips of branches (fireblight on a callery pear shown here). Try to remove at least 12 inches of branch tissue below the symptom and disinfest tools between cuts.

Diseased Branches – Cankers (top left)

Cankers may be identified by killing of the bark on a stem leaving sunken or swollen areas around the canker. Decay may also be present in these cankers. Try to prune at least 12 inches below the canker and disinfest pruning tools after the pruning cut.

Diseased Branches – Decay (top right)

Decay may be identified by the erosion or rotting of branch or stem tissues. Decayed branches should be removed.

Diseased Branches – Galls

Galls may be identified by large swollen areas of the branch tissue (black knot on a cherry tree shown here). Try to prune at least 12 inches below the gall and disinfest pruning tools after the pruning cut.

Remove the less dominant or less desirable of rubbing branches.

B – Bad Branch Attachments

Bad branch attachments have an increased potential to break or fail, and this may shorten the life of the tree. Bad attachments are identified by a narrow angle of attachment (termed a V-crotch) between a branch and its parent, along with several additional indicators. The presence of bark trapped between the branch and its parent (included bark) greatly increases the potential for bad branch attachments to break.

OBJECTIVE

▶ Learn how to identify the characteristics of bad and strong branch attachments.

▶ Learn how to prune branches with bad branch attachments.

APPLICATION

Identify bad branch attachments by:

▶ Narrow or V-shaped angle between the branch and parent and

- A seam between the branch and parent instead of the branch bark ridge.
- Swelling may be present at the base of the seam.

Stronger attachments are formed by:

▶ Wider angle of attachments or U-shaped angles.

▶ Presence of a branch bark ridge.

▶ The diameter of the lateral branch is less than ½ the diameter of the parent at the attachment.

Remove or suppress bad branch attachments:

▶ Start with the largest branches, lowest on the tree.

▶ Use reduction or heading cuts to avoid over-dosing if there are many branches with bad branch attachments.

▶ Do not completely remove branches that are directly next to each other or above/below each other. Instead, use a reduction or heading cut on one of the branches.

Measure your pruning dose by placing each branch pruned in a single pile and quantify the percentage of live crown removed.

▶ Stop pruning once dose is reached, or proceed to the next branch or step if dose has not been reached.

The left branch has narrow angle or a V-shaped attachment and a seam instead of a branch bark ridge. This attachment is considered a bad branch attachment because it is weakly attached to the parent branch. The branch on the right has a wider angle of attachment with the branch bark ridge evident and is a stronger attachment.

A bad branch attachment. Note the swelling at the base of the seam.

Bark (circle) that was included or trapped between two codominant stems. The inclusion weakens the branch attachment and resulted in this branch failing later in the life of this tree.

C – Competing Branches – Clearance/Branching Height

Clearance includes branches that are competing for space or conflicting with people, structures, vehicles or equipment.

Branching height is the distance from the ground to the lowest branch on the tree. Pruning lower branches may be required to reach a desired branching height. The desired branching height is a personal decision, but is also limited by how tall the tree species you are pruning can grow and its landscape location. Some trees, particularly ornamentals, may be left with branches low on the trunk or with multiple trunks to achieve a desired aesthetic objective.

OBJECTIVE

▶ Identify and prune branches on the tree that are creating clearance issues and work to achieve a desired branching height for the tree. *(See Section E for common pruning scenarios where branching height is adapted to personal preferences and location needs.)*

APPLICATION

Branching Height

▶ Remove branches in the bottom ¼ to ⅓ of the tree's total height or to a desired branching height below ¼ to ⅓ of the tree's total height.

   • Do not remove two or more branches immediately next to one another, either vertically or horizontally.

      – Remove one and use reduction or heading cuts on the other(s) to suppress growth, and plan on removing them in future pruning events.

▶ Remove or head sprouts on the trunk.

   • Leave some sprouts if:
      – There is an adjacent wound or
      – There is prolific sprouting on the trunk or
      – The tree was planted within the last three years.

APPLICATION continued

Clearance

▶ Reduce or head branches that are causing clearance issues above ¼ to ⅓ the height of the tree.

- Clearance over sidewalks is generally 8 to 10 feet, 13 to 15 feet over roadways; and as needed for lighting and specific lawn or other maintenance equipment.

Measure your pruning dose by placing each branch pruned in a single pile and quantify the percentage of live crown removed.

▶ Stop pruning once dose is reached, or proceed to the next branch or step if dose has not been reached.

Continued on next page.

Branching Height

Remove branches below ¼ to ⅓ the height of the tree. Do not remove two branches that are directly above or next each other on the trunk during the same pruning event.

Branching Height

Branching height is also a personal or aesthetic decision that depends on the tree species and location. Beech trees are commonly left with low branches on the trunk.

Remove some sprouts on the trunk. If there are multiple sprouts remove one and suppress the others. Sprouting can be a symptom of stress and removing them all may result in re-sprouting.

Clearance

A lateral branch that conflicted with pedestrians but was too large to remove was reduced to suppress its growth It should be removed at a later pruning event. Use reduction or heading cuts on branches that are conflicting and are above ¼ to ⅓ the height of the tree.

C – Codominant Stems

Several different types of competing branches are presented in the remainder of Step C in order of importance for pruning. First are codominant stems, two stems that are attached at the same point on the central stem and are competing with each other for apical dominance.

OBJECTIVE

▶ Identify and prune any codominant stems present on the central stem.

▶ Determine the type of pruning cut to be used on each codominant stem.

APPLICATION

Identify all codominant stems.

▶ Select one of the stems to serve as the central stem (if the tree is an A-Form).

▶ Suppress or remove any codominant stems competing with the central stem.

▶ If multiple codominant stems exist:

• Prune in order of branch size (diameter), starting with the largest to the smallest codominants until dose is reached.

• Use reduction or heading cuts if dose might be exceeded by removing a codominant stem, or if the branch is too large to remove all at once.

• Severely suppress or be sure to remove at least ⅓ to ¾ the live branch area on codominant branches that will eventually be removed.

Measure your pruning dose by placing each branch pruned in a single pile and quantify the percentage of live crown removed.

▶ Stop pruning once dose is reached, or proceed to the next branch or step if dose has not been reached.

Codominant stems split apart on this mature honeylocust. Codominant stems become a structural weakness that eventually may fail and shorten the lifespan of the tree.

Prune codominant stems competing for apical dominance starting with the largest and finishing with the smallest. Select one to serve as the central stem and remove or suppress the other. In this case, choose the more dominant of the two (larger diameter) to serve as the central stem (white line).

Removal cut being used on a codominant stem. Reduction or heading cuts can also be used on codominant stems if dose will be exceeded by using a removal cut.

Codominant stems on this Norway maple require pruning before they become too large and are difficult to correct without disfiguring the tree.

Conifers can also produce codominant stems. Select one to serve as the central stem and prune the others.

C – Competing Laterals

Competing laterals are branches that compete with the central stem by virtue of:

▶ Their fast upward growth or

▶ Their size, unbalancing the crown or

▶ Their large diameter relative to the parent or central stem.

OBJECTIVE

▶ To identify and prune any competing lateral branches.

APPLICATION

Identify and remove or suppress:

▶ Branches that are contributing to an unbalanced crown because of their large size or upward growth.

  • Suppress upward-directed laterals competing with the central stem.

▶ Branches that are more than ½ the diameter of the parent where they attach.

  • Use reduction or heading cuts to suppress these branches.

  • B-Form Trees – horizontally growing scaffold branches develop the natural growth form of the tree and this issue becomes less important. Allow these branches to grow once the tree reaches desired branching height.

Measure your pruning dose by placing each branch pruned in a single pile and quantify the percentage of live crown removed.

▶ Stop pruning once dose is reached, or proceed to the next branch or step if dose has not been reached.

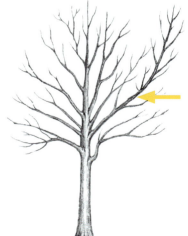

Competing lateral (arrow) may make the tree aesthetically unbalanced and they compete with the central stem for apical dominance.

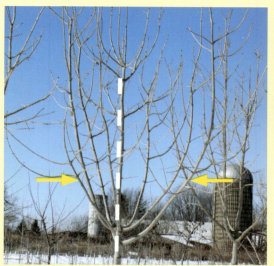

Fast upward-growing competing laterals on this maple (arrows) are competing with the central stem (white line) for apical dominance. Suppress or remove competing laterals.

Competing lateral by virtue of its size relative to the parent or central stem. Ideally, the diameter of a lateral branch should not exceed ½ the diameter of the trunk. The V-shaped branch union also constitutes a bad branch attachment.

B-Form Ornamental Tree
Note the several larger diameter scaffold branches growing laterally giving the tree its form. As ornamental tree species mature, horizontally growing scaffold branches such as these develop the natural growth form of the tree and the competing lateral issue becomes less important. Allow these branches to grow once you have reached the desired branching height on the tree.

This competing lateral is being suppressed with reduction and heading cuts because it is too large to remove at this time. It will be completely removed at a later pruning event.

C – Multiple Attachments – Horizontal Spacing

Multiple branch attachments are groups of two or more branches that are attached in the same or nearly the same horizontal plane or location around the central stem.

OBJECTIVE

▶ Identify and prune to correct multiple branch attachments and improve horizontal spacing around the central stem.

APPLICATION

Identify and prune multiple branch attachments present on the central stem.

▶ B-Form, "V-shaped" trees – <u>skip</u> this step.

▶ With A-Form trees, begin with groups of multiple attachments that are lowest on the central stem first.

▶ Identify one branch from each group of multiple attachments to be preserved.

  • Select one with good branch attachment, size relative to the central stem, and growing in a desirable direction.

  • Prune the largest diameter branches to be removed within a group first.

    – Ideally, remove one branch and suppress the other branches competing with your branch to be preserved.

    – Do not completely remove two branches that are directly next to each other or above/below each other.

    – Consider the impact on branches above (vertical spacing-next step) before pruning any branch for horizontal spacing.

▶ Move up the tree to the next group of horizontal branches for pruning if dose is not reached.

Measure your pruning dose by placing each branch pruned in a single pile and quantify the percentage of live crown removed.

▶ Stop pruning once dose is reached, or proceed to the next branch or step if dose has not been reached.

Start with lowest whorl and work up the central stem. Select a branch for preservation (blue arrows), remove one of the larger branches (red arrows) in the whorl and suppress the remaining (yellow arrow).

Multiple branch attachments – this maple has two whorls of two branches originating from the same horizontal point on the central stem. Select one branch to preserve in a whorl and remove or suppress one of the branches.

In most cases, it is best to prune the larger of the two branches.

Skip this and the next step (Vertical Spacing) on most B-Form, "V-shaped" trees, like this zelkova, that naturally form multiple attachments. They will be addressed in the ABCs by pruning bad branches, codominant branch attachments, and crossing and rubbing branches.

C – Vertical Spacing

Vertical spacing is the distance between individual branches as you move up the central stem. Branches that are attached at nearly the same vertical point on the central stem will grow in diameter and size, and crowd one another for space.

OBJECTIVE

▶ Improve vertical spacing of branches on the central stem.

APPLICATION

Identify branches whose branch attachments are touching or nearly touching at the same vertical point as you move up, down and around the central stem for pruning.

▶ B-Form, "V-shaped" trees – <u>skip</u> this step.

▶ For A-Form trees – begin with the lowest branches on the central stem and work your way up the central stem.

- Select the most desirable branches that will form an alternating or spiral pattern as you move up the central stem.

  – Remove or suppress the competing branches.

  – Do not remove any branch directly above or adjacent to another branch that has already been removed.

  – If necessary, use reduction or heading cuts to suppress a branch for removal at a later pruning event.

Measure your pruning dose by placing each branch pruned in a single pile and quantify the percentage of live crown removed.

▶ Stop pruning once dose is reached, or proceed to the next branch or step if dose has not been reached.

Vertical spacing is the spacing between branch attachments (yellow arrow) as you move up and down the central stem (white arrow).

In this case, the larger and lower of the two branches was removed to improve vertical spacing.

Vertical spacing pruning also requires observing branch attachments around the trunk. The middle branch is attached at nearly the same vertical point on the trunk with the branches on the upper left and lower right (yellow arrows).

To increase vertical spacing with the branches on the left and right (yellow arrows), the middle branch was removed.

C – Crossing Branches

Crossing branches are those that are overlapping or crossing but are not yet touching. With time, crossing branches usually will result in rubbing branches. In most cases, one of the crossing branches is growing in an undesirable direction and can be removed.

OBJECTIVE

▶ Identify and remove crossing branches before they increase in size and cause damage to other more desirable branches.

APPLICATION

Identify and prune undesirable crossing branches, including:

▶ Crossing laterals.

▶ Sprouts or upward-growing shoots on lateral branches.

If possible, use a removal cut to eliminate the less desirable of the crossing branches.

▶ Suppress the less desirable crossing branch if removal is not appropriate.

Measure your pruning dose by placing each branch pruned in a single pile and quantify the percentage of live crown removed.

▶ Stop pruning once dose is reached, or proceed to the next branch or step if dose has not been reached.

Crossing laterals that will eventually rub a more desirable branch should be removed.

Upward growing branches or sprouts conflict with other more desirable branches and should be removed.

Other Important Pruning Tips

Section D | Other Important Pruning Tips

Timing of Pruning

Trees can be pruned at any time of the year, but:

▶ Some periods are better than others.

▶ Timing will affect growth response.

OBJECTIVE

▶ Determine the best time to prune based on the pruning objective or objectives.

APPLICATION

<u>It is ideal and easiest to prune in the winter</u> when the leaves are off the trees, revealing the branching structure of the tree. The winter season is also better because tree pests are less active. The late spring and summer months are the next best time to prune, although pruning should be avoided during periods of prolonged drought unless supplemental watering is supplied to the tree. Dead, broken or pest-infected branches can be pruned any time of the year.

Spring pruning should be avoided because significant physiologic changes are occurring in the tree as buds and twigs are expanding and beginning to grow.

There are additional pruning objectives to consider and can be found in Table 1. Weigh the importance of those objectives to help you decide the best time to prune.

Table 1.
Importance of time of year of pruning on growth, flowering and response of trees.

Objective/ Issue	Timing to Prune	Comment
Health/Structure/Ease	1-Winter, 2-Summer	Winter is ideal followed by summer
Showy flowers and fruit	After flowering	Pruning before flowering removes flower buds
Increase fruit size	Prior to flowering	Reduces the number of flowers and thus fruit will become larger, pruning for fruit production is not addressed in this book
Reduce Sprouting	Summer	Reduces current year sprouting
Fast wound closure	Early to mid-summer	Wound closure can be delayed by dormant pruning
Wound bleeding on some species such as maples and birches	Avoid late winter/ early spring	Wounds will "bleed" sap excessively; bleeding is not considered harmful
Bark ripping	Avoid the weeks just before and after bud break	Tender or slippery bark that may tear when making cuts. Some species such as elms have slippery bark well into the spring

Pruning Interval

Pruning interval is defined as the number of years between each time the tree is pruned (a pruning event). Other than pruning to remove dead, broken or pest-infested branches, a tree should not be pruned more than once in a growing season if a full dose was removed from the tree.

OBJECTIVE

▶ Determine the pruning interval based on the tree's pruning needs.

APPLICATION

The standard pruning interval recommended for young trees is three years. However, shorter pruning intervals allow one to intervene and correct neglected trees and proactively direct growth.

▶ Use pruning intervals of less than three years for trees:

- That are growing vigorously (twig growth increments greater than one foot per year),
- Require extensive pruning to correct branch defects,
- When you have the ability to visit the tree frequently.
  - Dose should be reduced at each pruning event.

Do not exceed dose on any tree, no matter what the pruning interval.

Pruning interval is the number of years between pruning events. Shorter pruning intervals may be needed to correct serious structural problems such as these multiple branch attachments on this callery pear.

Tree species, age and growth rate may affect the pruning interval selected. Fast growing species such as the hybrid elm shown here may require a more frequent pruning interval to intervene and direct growth.

Dead, dying, pest-infested or diseased branches can be pruned at any time.

Dose should be minimized and a pruning interval of at least three years should be used on these recently transplanted, low vigor maples until their health improves.

Pruning Wound Dressing and Treatments

Paints, shellacs, asphalts and other dressings and wraps applied to pruning wounds (or other wounds) are called wound dressings. The purpose of these treatments is an attempt to protect wounds from infection by pathogens, invasion by insects and to increase the rate of wound closure. Based on current research, wound dressings are generally not recommended as some dressings may be toxic to the tree or may slow wound closure, and have not been shown to protect wounds from disease or insects.

OBJECTIVE
Learn alternative methods to avoid using wound dressing.

APPLICATION
Do not use wound dressings on wounds. The following reasons are often cited for using wound dressings. Alternatives to dressings for achieving the stated reason are provided.

Table 2.
Alternative methods to avoid the use of wound dressings.

Objective	Use or Alternative
Fast wound closure	Prune during growing season. Remove large diameter branches over a number of pruning events with reduction or heading cuts.
Aesthetics	Prune fewer branches and smaller diameter branches on a shorter pruning interval.
Avoid pruning wound bleeding	Do not prune susceptible species in later winter (Table 1).
Promote wound closure	Promote good tree health through good Plant Health Care management practices such as mulching, watering, and fertility.

Treatment of pruning wounds with paints or other wound treatments are usually not recommended because in most cases these treatments have not been found effective in stopping decay or other diseases.

Pruning wound "bleeding" can be avoided by not pruning susceptible species such as this maple in late winter.

A proper pruning cut made when a branch is small is the best treatment to avoid pest problems resulting from pruning. Small wounds on young, healthy trees will close quickly and will usually leave a nearly symmetrical circle of wound wood growth around the pruning cut.

The DON'TS of Tree Pruning

Poor pruning practices can have short and long-term negative impacts on tree health. This section identifies several of the most common poor pruning practices.

OBJECTIVE

▶ Learn what the most common improper pruning practices look like so they can be avoided when using the ABCs method.

D – Over Dose
Don't prune more than the prescribed dose.

N – Never Flush Cut
A flush cut is a final cut that cuts the branch bark ridge and branch collar, "flush" with the parent and causes unnecessary damage to the parent. Flush cuts will leave an unsymmetrical often "eye" shaped woundwood around the wound.

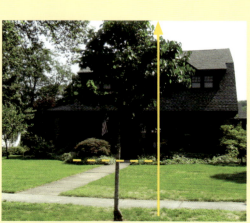

O – Over Raising
Don't remove all the branches from the trunk above ¼ to ⅓ the height of the tree.

N – Never Rip
A "ripped" pruning cut results in a large wound damaging the parent. Use the three-step method to help avoid this type of damage to the tree. Note a chainsaw was used and resulted in cutting the parent.

T – Tools

Don't use the wrong tool or a dull tool for making a pruning cut. Here, a chainsaw was used to cut this small branch resulting in damage to the parent, ripping and a flush cut.

T – Top or Lions Tail

Topping is the indiscriminate removal of the terminal portions of all the branches on a tree. It results is prolific weakly attached sprouting and wounding that is slow to seal. Lions tailing is the practice of removing all of the interior laterals and leaving the laterals at the end of the parent resulting in the branch having a "lion's tail" appearance.

S – Stub

A stub left after a removal cut. Leaving a stub slows the rate for wound closure and provides an avenue for pests to enter the parent.

Section E

Extras

Section E | Extras

Determining a Branching Height

Branching height is the distance from the ground to the lowest branch on a tree. Most young trees will have the branches in the lower ¼ to ⅓ of the height of the tree removed as the tree matures. This pruning will stop when the desired branching height is achieved. The branching height of a tree is determined by its location in the landscape, personal preferences and ultimately the height the tree will reach at maturity.

OBJECTIVE

▶   Determine a branching height of a tree.

APPLICATION

▶   Observe the location of the tree in the landscape.
   • Does the location of the tree dictate the removal of branches low on the tree to accommodate the safe passage of people or equipment under the tree or clearance from permanent structures or other plants?

▶   Low Branched Tree – There is suitable space for tree to grow in height and spread without conflict and you would like to keep the tree low branched.
   • In most cases it is best to remove any branch that is touching the ground.
   • Maintain mulch under the tree from the trunk to outside the spread of branches.

▶   Raised Branched Tree – Tree must have suitable space for people and motor vehicles to safely pass under the tree or clearance from permanent structures or other plants.
   • Branches low on the tree will need to be removed over multiple pruning events.
   • Remove branches in the lower ¼ to ⅓ the height of the tree until a desired branching height is achieved.

   • Different sides of the tree can have different branching heights depending on the activities or structures under them.
   • Use reduction or heading cuts on conflicting branches above ¼ to ⅓ the height of the tree.

Determining branching height is a decision that is based on the present height of the tree and placement of the tree in the landscape. Evaluate the location of the tree in the landscape to determine if the tree can remain as a Low Branched Tree or must be pruned as a Raised Branched Tree.

Low Branched Tree – Lawn Area
This beech tree has been left with branches low on the trunk. Maintain mulch or plant ground cover as shown here, under the entire spread of the tree to protect the lower branches from damage.

Low Branched Tree – Planting Bed
The owner has chosen to maintain this ornamental tree low branched to achieve a desired aesthetic design.

Raised Branch Tree – Lawn Area
This maple tree located in a lawn area, near a sidewalk, will require pruning of low branches to provide suitable space for people and lawn equipment to pass under the tree without interference.

In no case should you remove branches above ¼ to ⅓ of the height of the tree. Branches that are creating clearance issues above this height should be pruned with heading or reduction cuts.

Raised Branched Tree – Planting Bed Hawthorns located in a planting bed have had lower branches pruned to accommodate shrubs under the trees.

Raised Branch Tree – Street Trees These magnolias on the right are mature and lower branches cannot be removed. Clearance issues will have to be addressed using reduction and heading cuts.

Raised Branched Tree – Street Tree
This maple tree will require pruning of lower branches over the sidewalk and ultimately over the street when the tree matures.

Using the ABCs – Before and Afters

Hackberry – poor health, A-Form. A low dose was prescribed and pruning primarily included A – apical dominance and a removal cut of a C – competing lateral.

Green ash – good health, A-Form. The majority of the dose was used to prune for A–apical dominance and C – competing branches on the lower portion of the trunk.

Littleleaf linden - poor health, A-Form. A low dose was prescribed and pruning primarily included A – apical dominance and B – bad branches.

Green ash – good health, A-Form. A normal dose was prescribed and pruning primarily included A – apical dominance and C – clearance and competing laterals.

Hackberry – good health, A-Form. A normal dose was prescribed and pruning included: A – apical dominance and C – clearance and competing laterals.

Crabapple – good health, B-Form. A normal dose was prescribed and pruning included removing B – rubbing branches and suppressing the C-competing lateral on the left side of the tree.

Coffee Tree – good health, A-Form. A normal dose was used to prune for A – apical dominance and C – competing lateral.

Hawthorn – good health, B-Form. A normal dose was prescribed and pruning primarily included B – rubbing branches and C – clearance.

ABCs Credits

Book Review
Sam Bishop, Trees NY, New York NY
Jerry Bond, Urban Forest Analytics, Geneva, NY
Larry Costello, University of California/Davis, Davis, CA
Beverly Gibson, Yankee Gardener, Webster, NY
Ed Gilman, University of Florida, Gainesville, FL
Jack Ritz, Rochester, NY
Tom Ritz, City of Rochester Forestry Division, Rochester, NY
Berna Ticonchuk, Finger Lakes Community College, Canandaigua, NY

Book Design & Layout
Shelly Dinan, Dinan Communications, Rochester NY

Illustrations
Nancy Lane, Nancy Lane Studios, Canandaigua, NY

Trees To Illustrate The ABCs of Pruning
Chris Dorn, City of Canandaigua, Canandaigua, NY